Life Can

Be Cruel

BY

H. R. R. FURMANSKI

VANTAGE PRESS   NEW YORK   WASHINGTON   HOLLYWOOD

FIRST EDITION

Copyright, 1960, by H. R. R. Furmanski

Published by Vantage Press, Inc.
120 West 31st Street, New York 1, N. Y.

Manufactured in the United States of America

My thanks to Rebecca Bloomfield
for encouraging me
to write this book

Life Can

Be Cruel

I was born in a small town in East Prussia, on a bitter cold night in January. The year was 1913, one year before the outbreak of World War I. My parents were very happy and proud that their second child was a boy. At last, thought Papa, I will have a male heir who can carry on the business and keep alive the family tradition. In his mind he was already planning my future. With fatherly pride he bent to kiss my mother and thank her for giving him a son. It had been a long time between children—thirteen years—and although Papa loved my sister Frieda and gave her the best which he was able to provide, still, she was only a girl, and a girl did not share the pride of her father's profession in those days, nor did she hold the promise of a new and more prosperous generation that would bear the family name. All of this was important to Papa, who was a proud, strong-willed man, a master pastry chef who took pride in his craft.

His mouth was a firm line separating a determined chin and a carefully trimmed black mustache. I cannot recall those set features ever changing, nor the mustache being any color but a shiny, bristly black, though I know that, as he grew older, his face became lined, and his hair turned gray.

I do not mean to imply that Papa was a vain man. No, he simply took a craftsman's pride in his work, and he found in the prospect of a son to follow him a new energy, a new incentive—and he worked doubly hard. His well-established pastry shop flourished and prospered under his constant supervision and his contagious, driving spirit.

No matter how loudly or how often the bell on the shop door rang, Papa's voice could be heard throughout the kitchen. No matter how thickly the dust of flour filled the air, Papa's quick, deep eyes mirrored his mood—an occasional displeasure or, more often, the deep pleasure experienced by a man who has given of his best and whose work has met with approval.

And so, with the birth of a son into the family, business seemed to thrive to an even greater extent. New customers flocked to the bakery, and soon the kitchens were expanded and modernized. The cash register played a merry tune, and life was full for my papa. And yet, it is not Papa whom I remember most clearly. When I think of the shop and the counter that sat spotlessly clean before the customers, and the wonderful smells that came from the lovely products of my father's art, I see Mother. Mother—I never called her Mama or Mummy or Ma. These words were just sounds to me— empty terms of endearment that any child could push from between baby lips to call any woman who was kind to him or gave him pretty things. But Mother was more than a word or a woman who showed me great kindness: she wove her soul into mine with careful, firm stitches that formed patterns of goodness and love, comfort and security, understanding and peace. I cannot tell now where her soul ended and mine began.

Looking back in memory, I see her in the shop as a slender, blond woman with deep blue eyes. I remember the smile that seemed never to leave her lips, and the happy words that were always on her tongue as she waited on friends and strangers in the store. I remember how she would come to me in her free moments from the shop, wearing her apron, the warm smell of baked goods clinging to her person. And I remember how she prayed with me and for me, through all the busy days between shop and home, through all the painful days of childhood sickness and shattered dreams, through all the blackened days when war sounds drowned her words to my ears. At no time was I unaware of her presence.

My first year was therefore spent in a wonderfully peaceful and secure atmosphere. We had enough on which to live, enough room in which to be happy, and enough love shared among us to teach us to love life. Never were strong words or quarrels heard in our house, for Mother and Papa preserved the sanctity of their home, as though the home were an entity in itself, and yet deeply and profoundly a part of each of us.

Then—quite without warning—even I, in my baby mind, could sense that something was wrong, was missing from our home. Frieda was with me constantly, and I waited eagerly for her to come to me in the morning and take me shopping for groceries, or for a walk down by the river that ran past our house, or to the dry-goods store to buy material for clothes. I loved the bright patterns of the cheap cotton and would sit fascinated as I followed the crazy designs that ran up and down the bolts of cloth. Mother would come in for lunch, but she no longer spent so much time with us, and though her eyes seemed to be trying very hard to smile, they never quite succeeded in covering the look of weariness and concern in her face.

During the afternoons I'd sit at the piano with Frieda and listen to her play, laughing at the silly little songs she made up for me and sitting solemnly silent as her fingers ran across the keys in a Bach sonata or a section of a Beethoven symphony. Mother would be there for supper too, and for a little play before bedtime. Then the lack became apparent to me, for while Mother and Frieda were always near me, their love with me always, Papa was gone. That was where the emptiness came from; that's what was missing. And suddenly I asked, "Where is Papa? Why is his place empty at our supper table?"

Mother told me calmly that Papa had to go to war with the other men, and that we must wait patiently until it was time for him to come home. No, she didn't know when that time would be, we must not doubt that he would come home, and in the meantime we must be good and wait for him. I felt a great hatred for this "war," not because I knew what war was exactly or that it could prevent Papa from ever coming home: I hated it because war was a place or a thing or a person that kept my father from me and made Frieda solemn and Mother sad and tired whenever it was mentioned.

For four years I listened to the word and could pick out the letters in the print of the newspapers—and I hated it more and more.

My mother worked hard to keep the kitchen in the bake- · shop busy, the books balanced, and the building that housed our home exactly as it was before—before the war. She never complained, never whined, never let anyone know how she felt inside. At night, when we prayed together—Mother, Frieda, and I—she would always thank God that we could share all the blessings that he had given us, humbly asking that her husband be returned safely to his family.

And it was in this manner that we lived through the days. Spring came late, that year of 1918: even the seasons seemed to be waiting for the war to end, as though the world wanted to wait for a peaceful atmosphere before exhibiting the beauty that can only be enjoyed in time of peace. The river that ran past our house was still frozen, and it looked as if it would never melt. Frieda warned me that the ice really wasn't as strong as it looked, but I told her not to be silly, that if I still had to bundle up in so many sweaters and mufflers then it certainly was cold enough to go sliding on the ice with the other children without fear of the ice melting.

"If I fall through the ice, it will be because all this clothing has made me as heavy as the blacksmith's anvil, and that *surely* would fall through the ice," I laughingly chided, and shuffled out the door to join the others.

Darkness began to descend at its early winter hour. The older children reluctantly acknowledged the lighting of the streetlamps, called younger sisters, brothers, and neighbors' children who were in their charge, leaving only a few of us behind. I hadn't noticed their departure, nor did I notice that the others were slowly leaving too. Frieda had learned a lovely new piece of music, and I was intent on fitting the rhythm of my slide dance to the new melody humming it over and over again. I glided back and forth and in patterns, listening to the sound of the slide and stopping when that sound seemed in discord with the melody that ran through my mind in pleasant repetition. It wasn't a dance, really— just an exercise, a game I played that gave me great pleasure and shut off the street and the houses and the shop and all sense of time and area. Taking a run on the trill and sliding until the melody ended, I thought: I'll wager I can slide all the way to the end of this theme if I get a good start. Start— *slide*—the trill—*slide*—take the run and—here comes the melody—*slide, slide, slide*—Wait, I thought, that's not the sound of a slide—what is it? Stop, stop—you're falling—it's the ice—it's cracking and melting. Wait, don't let yourself fall—stop it, stop it! Just yell, yell for Mother—Mother— yell for Frieda. Go ahead, the words are in your mind—put them in your mouth—yell for help. I can't, I thought. I can't yell for anybody. It's too late. I've fallen, and the water is all around. It's cold. It's so cold that I can't yell; I can't scream. Water, cold water. Look, I told myself, you're all right. It's only cold water, and it's near the edge of the river. Climb out. Hurry—hurry before anyone sees and tells Mother. No, don't cry. Pull the other leg up and run some place before Frieda comes looking for you. Papa wouldn't cry. Frieda doesn't— all right, I've stopped crying. There wasn't even any need to cry because I didn't fall in all the way, I thought. You're all wet though, I told myself. And Frieda told you not to go sliding. She'll be angry with you, and Mother will know right away; she'll be disappointed. You should have listened to

13

Frieda. But everyone else came out to slide, I reminded my-self. If everyone else came, why couldn't I?

But you stayed too long, I told myself. It's almost dark, and you should be home getting ready for dinner. And don't cry. Papa had to go to war, and he didn't—I'm not crying, I thought. I'm only sniffling because my nose is dripping from the water. I didn't mean to stay so late. Nobody came and told me to come home. Christel usually tells me when it's time, but she didn't, and—no, I'm not crying: I'm only sniffling—like Mother does sometimes. Mother has to work very hard and— But you're all wet, I reminded myself; how are you going to tell Mother that you forgot it was time to come home and have dinner with her? She will be disappointed, and your clothes are all wet, soaked clear through. You can't go home in wet clothes. I'll dry them off, I thought; she won't be so angry if I dry them off. I'll run to Christel's papa's barn and wait until they dry off. Hurry, hurry. Run to the barn. Don't sniffle so badly—run. No, no, don't drag your feet—that makes noise. Just run. But I can't feel my feet, I protested. I don't know that I'm dragging them, because I can't feel them. They must be dry . . . and yet I can feel the squish of the water in my socks and the heaviness of the wet cuff.

Run, run to the barn, I thought doggedly. No, don't cough; you'll make noise, and they'll hear you. Just go a little farther and you will be at the barn. And don't sniffle. I can't help it, I replied—I can't stop sniffling. I think I should go home. I don't want to stay at the barn. Everything must be dry; it doesn't feel wet any more. It feels as heavy as when I left the house—such a long time ago. I must be dry. I'll go home now. But I'll walk slowly because I have to stop sniffling and coughing. That's funny—I was so cold before and now I'm not cold at all, except for a little chill once in a while. I'm warm; in fact, I'm hot. I'll just apologize to Mother for being late. I won't tell her I fell in the river. I'll stop sniffling soon, and I won't cough. What are you going to say? I asked my-self. You're almost home. You'd better practice out loud what you're going to say, so you'll be sure not to cough. Come on, clear your throat and talk. Hurry, hurry. Clear your throat and practice what you're going to say. You're at the door now; it's too late to practice. Don't be afraid—it's not a lie that you're going to tell—and don't sniffle. Just tell Mother and Frieda that—

But I didn't have to tell Mother and Frieda anything. As soon as I entered the house I began to cry hysterically, and they ran to me. I'm sure I told them nothing of what had happened: breathing was so difficult that I found myself un-able to talk. They quickly carried me upstairs. The clothes that I thought had dried were frozen on me, and the buttons were so brittle that they broke right off. Mother and Frieda worked with an urgency that even I could feel. Mother's hands worked quickly and steadily as she undressed me, but her voice was sweet and smooth and forgiving, except when she'd whisper something to Frieda.

I wasn't crying any more: I had to use all my energy to breathe now. And I didn't think about apologizing, for my head was throbbing so loudly that I was unable to think. My whole body was fighting to catch the air and draw it into my lungs—fighting to shut out the horrible, steady sound of the throb that boomed in the depths of my skull and threatened to break through my temples.

Mother sat with me for a long time, I remember, and tried to ease the pain and lower the fever. I don't know exactly how long she was there, for I fell into a deep, horrible night-mare. In my delirium I saw the ice topple over me, and I struggled violently to stop it, so violently that I lost my breath and had to fight to get it back. When I stopped to breathe, the ice gave way, and I fell and fell down to the bottom of the river. There was a great fish, and his name was

"War," and he had swallowed Papa, just as he was going to swallow me. I ran out of air and was surely going to drown. I swam with all my might, flailing my arms and churning my legs to push back the water and reach the surface before my lungs burst. But the fish called War kept following me, and from his mouth came the sounds of Frieda's piano, and I knew he had swallowed her, too; but I couldn't get out of the water, and I couldn't turn around to save Papa and Frieda, and the current kept carrying me along with the big fish right behind, so that I couldn't stop for a moment to find a way out.

The dream went on this way, repeating itself for three days, though I myself had lost track of time. At times it seemed as if the story had played itself for the last time, and I would see Frieda and Mother sitting by my bed, and I would try to tell them that I had fallen through the ice and was having a terrible dream, and that they should go to bed because I was all right now. But the words never came, and I would listen to Frieda speaking to me and try to drink what she gave me, or watch Mother praying next to me with the flour still on her hands and her apron still tied around her. I would try to smile and tell her that everything was all right, but then I'd be afraid again. The breathing would become more difficult. The throbbing in my head turned into the sound of crashing ice, and I would be lost in the same hideous fantasy.

Then on the morning of the third day I fell into what seemed to be a deep sleep. Mother rested, and Frieda whispered to those in the shop that everything was going to be all right. All day long we slept, Mother and I, and she rose in the evening to eat, and then came in to feed me. But I didn't wake from the deep comatose state that held me in so tight a grip. She gently placed her hand under me and tried to lift me, but I began to choke, and she laid me gently back on the pillows. The choking sound that came from my throat didn't stop, and the sound frightened Frieda into tears. Mother was frightened too. She watched the small body as it struggled to catch the air to swallow it, to dislodge the web that was knitting itself across the windpipe. Then she shook herself from her fright and moved quickly.

"Get my wrap," she whispered hastily to Frieda while she began wrapping me in blankets. She slipped on her coat, picked me up swiftly, and ran out of the house, holding her bundle tightly. She must have looked very strange, running down the street—like a mad woman or a thief—but a second look would have made it apparent to those who watched that she ran with urgent and deliberate steps toward the hospital.

The hospital was a big red stone building located a few blocks away from our home, large and well equipped as compared with other hospitals in Germany in 1918, since our town was the county seat of an important section. But it was badly understaffed, which was not unusual in that wartime year. Mother sent a nurse to find a doctor, but she wouldn't let me be taken from her: she followed the bustling white and gray figure, still clutching her bundle. When she saw the doctor, she stopped suddenly and looked at him in astonishment: he was only a boy. In fact, she knew him to be Joseph Henze, a neighbor's son. She laid me on the table and undid the blankets, talking while she did so, describing the course of the illness during the past two days. As she finished she straightened up, saying in a soft but firm voice, "He is very ill, Doctor, I know. But you must not let him die. He is only five years old, but he is the man of our house."

The young doctor smiled and began his examination. His look grew suddenly grave. "Your son has diphtheria," he said. "The diphtheria has knitted a web across his trachea— his windpipe through which he must breathe. I will tell them to prepare him for surgery. In two hours we can operate—if he is alive. If he is not, then our preparations did no harm, at any rate."

He looked at the woman to gauge her reaction. She said nothing, only nodding in acknowledgement of his words. She didn't cry or gasp or faint. She sat in a chair near her son's head and began her wait.

Joseph Henze whispered his instructions to the nurse and quickly left the room to prepare himself for the operation. He might have told the woman it was too late to do anything to save her son. This would have been very close to being the truth. He had never performed the operation before, and his staff was as young and inexperienced as he. The boy might die anyway. Yes, he might. The chance of shock afterward, and the daily risks incurred during the period of the boy's recuperation, might well kill him. Yet this woman expected him to save her son, and as long as there was a chance of his being able to do it, he must try. He would perform the operation—if the child lived through the next two hours. Suddenly he hoped—almost prayed—that the child would live so that he could prove to himself and them—the rest of the world that doubted his skill because of his youth and his idealism—that idealism was a form of determination, and that with determination he could save the boy and live up to his ideals.

For Doctor Henze the two hours passed all too quickly. For the woman in the small room each minute contained a sunrise and sunset, while the sound of the nurse's skirts and her son's choked breathing echoed like thunder in the walls of a canyon. She tried to quiet the tumult with her prayers, to bring peace to herself and her son. It was almost a relief when the doctor appeared, though she dreaded the surgery with a fear that was largely instinctive. The boy was still alive: they would operate. The small party moved toward the operating room. Dr. Henze explained that he was going to enter the boy's throat and find the web. He would then place a small tube in the trachea and remove the web through suction. He would leave the tube in, through which the last vestige of the web would have to be removed until there was no longer any danger of the web re-forming. 'If, he made it very clear, the boy survived the operation.

He assured her that he would do everything he could, but he knew that she didn't need his assurances. They both knew that the outcome was largely in the hands of God. And they both prayed.

The operation began. Slowly, and with great concentration, the doctor worked, constantly checking the pulse and temperature of the small body beneath his hands. Slowly, and with great emotion, the words of prayer formed in the mind of the woman outside. At times the image of her son and the image of her husband seemed to blend into one image, to become one in her mind. She could not lose both. She *would* not lose both. Her husband would return to find his family waiting for him—his wife, his daughter, and his son. She strove mightily to convince herself of this.

The boy's chances for survival were diminishing with the decrease of his pulse rate and the lowering of his body temperature. His heart began to falter. The sound of the straining muscle became weaker, less frequent, more strained. The doctor worked with increased concentration. The small muscle rested, and they waited silently for it to beat again, praying that it would, soundlessly urging it, willing it, to resume its normal function. The young surgeon never stopped working, his orders for instruments, his instructions to his assistants quiet and unceasing. The heart beat again, hesitantly, as if unsure of its right to function normally. The woman outside heard the heartbeat in the click of the clock that faced her; she heard it in the hollow tread of a doctor's footstep; she heard it in the steady thump of cart wheels rolling by. She waited, listened. There were only two sounds in the world for her—the sound of that heartbeat and the sound of the prayers that formed in her mind's voice: all others had been obliterated.

The man inside the operating room heard the heartbeat, too. He strained to catch it as he inserted the small silver tube into the boy's trachea. It seemed to beat more loudly as he cleared the strangling web; and as he began to close the wound it seemed to fill the room with the strains of a triumphal march, a hallelujah chorus as its background. His fingers worked automatically with the bandages, his mind attuned to the *lub-dub* sound within the small breast, transforming it in his mind to an equally rhythmic and steady *Thank God, Thank God*. . . .

The woman outside turned suddenly in her chair; the door next to her had opened. Her maternal instinct was aroused by the sudden picture of the tired young man who slowly pulled himself out of the doorway. He walked to her slowly; she didn't dare to ask him. He didn't—he couldn't—use words to tell her: he simply smiled with a tired mouth, nodded his perspiring head and told her with thankful, almost exultant eyes that they had brought it off. The boy was alive; he had survived the operation, and at the moment that was all that mattered.

For two days I lay in a comatose state, not moving when they removed the small tube each morning, afternoon, and night to clean it. I slept, not knowing that I was constantly being watched for signs of shock, for difficulty in breathing or for signs of awakening. On the third day I awoke for short periods of time. I tried to move, but found I could not. I tried to speak, to tell Mother that I was glad she was there, wherever we were, because I felt so funny all over. Then I would fall back into my half-drugged sleep.

Mother, in order to be with me, left the shop with almost no supervision for nearly four days, the books becoming hopelessly confused, the stock in need of replenishing, and the kitchen in a muddle. It had been difficult enough having to be in two different places before the operation; now she had to make her presence felt in three different buildings, all demanding her concern, concentration, and constant supervision.

It was on the third day after the operation, as she sat tiredly and heavily in the chair beside the hospital bed, that I awoke from a deep slumber. The young doctor stood beside her, as he did each day until it was time for her to leave. They spoke little; just the amenities passed between my worried mother and the young physician.

Today, when I awoke, they were in their places, and they began to move simultaneously as I opened my eyes and showed signs of being fully awake. My mother took my hand and spoke to me as the doctor stood behind me and deftly moved his fingers over the bandage. He smiled as my eyes met his, then introduced himself. As simply as possible he explained to me what had happened; then he told both of us what he was going to do. The tube would be removed for cleaning three times a day until they were sure that the web would not form again. The procedure would be painful, but I would get used to it after a while. The length of time until I would be able to leave the hospital would depend on my recuperative powers, my co-operation, and the will of God.

Now he was going to show me how to speak. He placed his fingers over the protruding end of the silver tube, hoping that I would be able to utter a sound, any sound that would show that the passage was not clogged and that the vocal chords had not been damaged.

"Speak to your mother," the doctor said.

I could feel myself becoming frightened. I clutched my mother's hand. Perhaps if the doctor would take his hand away from the tube, I would be able to speak—or so it seemed at that moment. I wanted to clear my throat: it was as though a large lump of food or phlegm were caught in my throat, making it difficult to breathe. Suddenly, in my panic to catch a breath, the sound came out: it was a gravelly, breathy "Oh, Moth-er"—but it was a sound. The doctor smiled and took his finger from the opening of the tube; he had said he would do it, and, by God, he had. It was only a matter of time until I would be completely well. Cheerfully, almost jubilantly, he talked to me, endeavoring to calm my fears, explaining that, to talk, I must place my finger over the end of the tube. This would force the air through the voice box instead of out through the hole in the protruding end of the silver tube. Gently he grasped my hand and guided the index finger toward the opening. I was conscious of my eyes widening, and of a sense of panic. The scream which formed in my throat would not come out. Something dreadful was at my throat and in my throat and down my neck. It was horrible, knowing it was there, knowing that there was a hole in my throat and that I could not breathe without the terrible tube. I put all my strength into an effort to pull my hand from the doctor's grasp.

"There, come now," Mother coaxed. "You want to be able to speak to me and to Frieda, don't you? Come now, *mein Liebchen*. The tube is not so bad: it has saved the life of the man of my family. And surely the man of my family would not be afraid to touch a small pipe." But no amount of coaxing or reasoning could induce me to close the end of the tube and speak.

A game of pantomime developed in the weeks to come, and though the doctor would have liked to see me exercise

22

by putting my finger on the tube and speaking, he never once forced me to do so. But, during the night, when I was alone, I tried very hard to speak some words. I would and could surprise my mother and the doctor. I had to stay almost nine months in the hospital, but my efforts were finally rewarded, and I was thankful to God and the doctor that I was able to survive the operation and once more speak normally.

My mother wept tears of joy, praising the Lord the day when I was able to come home. After a short period of time she received a letter from Father, stating that he too was coming home soon. A great sense of joy and gratitude pervaded our home. Germany had lost the war, but our family won a battle of life. Father came home, a tired and war-weary man, but happy to be with his family again. Mother had kept the business and house in order, and we took up our life as it had been before the war. Frieda graduated from school, and I started elementary school. Everything was going smoothly and according to plan. As a pupil, my grades were above the average, for I was interested in counting, writing, and reading, eager to learn about the facts of the universe— what made the day and the night, where the rain came from, and so on. My teacher was unusually attentive to my questions, and went to great pains to supply satisfactory answers.

After four years of elementary school my principal wrote a letter to my parents, suggesting that they send me to high school. In Germany attending high school is a privilege of which people of the middle class seldom avail themselves. My parents had their first arguments over this decision, but finally my father agreed with Mother that I should go. I finished my elementary school in the spring and was transferred to the Humanistic Gymnasium in my hometown. I was very happy, for I had made up my mind to be a medical doctor.

I studied very hard, hoping to demonstrate to my parents a part of my gratitude for being permitted to attend high school.

Besides all the general courses during my first year, I was required to learn Latin. Experiencing some difficulty with the language, I finally sought the help of my mother. Soon I understood the basic fundamentals and readily mastered the language. This period of instruction brought me even closer to my mother and deepened my admiration for her, not only because she had the patience to tutor me, but because she proved herself to be a great philosopher. My mother taught me to love and respect my neighbor as myself, ever to be an "eagle and not a crow." For the eagle, as she pointed out to me, flies alone, whereas the crow flies in a crowd.

My father, being a strong-willed man, taught me to do everything right and never to be afraid of anyone. This home training, coupled with the education I received at school, gave me strength and power in preparing for the daily life. The help of my mother, along with my natural eagerness to study, resulted in my being promoted from the sixth grade to the eighth in one year.

Besides Latin, I was required to study French and Greek, arithmetic, geometry, algebra, physics, chemistry, and mathematics. In those courses also my mother was a great help. I showed my gratitude and thanks to my mother by studying doubly hard. My desire to be a doctor was strengthened with each day I spent in school.

Boys and girls who reached the age of sixteen in our school were permitted to take lessons in dancing and formal etiquette on the dance floor. This was a very happy time for every one of us. Fortunately, I loved music and possessed a natural sense of rhythm, and the girls were happy to dance with me. After twenty lessons we held a public dance, so that our parents might observe the progress we had made.

The preparation for this event created great excitement in town, the mothers of all the boys and girls counseling them in matters of decorum and department, for this dance was the highlight of the social year.

The dance itself was held in the latter part of November. All who were to take part in this event arrived well ahead of time. The ball started with a polonaise. Each boy had to dance at least one dance with each girl. It was a picture to see the girls in their beautiful dresses, and the boys in their tuxedos whirl and glide to the rhythm of a good orchestra. The parents sat around the dance floor, proud and happy, following their offspring with smiling eyes. It was a time of great enjoyment, for all concerned. As I look back upon it in memory, I am again caught up in the enchantment of the evening.

After this social event I had still two more years of schooling. They were years which I thoroughly enjoyed, for the opportunity of attending the university upon my graduation and becoming a medical doctor seemed well within my grasp. I studied extremely hard during those last two years, passing my final examination with honors. My parents, though proud and happy, did not yet talk about my future. It was not until I asked to go to the university that I realized my father had already made his plan for my future: I was to be a baker. This decision was my first major disappointment in life, and I very nearly broke down. His explanation was that his trade needed educated men, too.

I had studied very hard, had lost many years of recreation and pleasure. My soul was filled with a bitterness which came perilously close to being hate. I was torn between love and hate for my parents. I could not understand their indifference to my desires.

Many nights I cried over what was happening to me. I was

compelled to learn my father's trade. I permitted him to teach me, swallowing my disappointment. During the time of my apprenticeship my own personality seemed to be lost as I followed my father's dictates and commands, outwardly content, inwardly miserable. I wore two faces, for I was constantly tormented by my dilemma. It was a hard and strange life for me, one which I failed to understand. I didn't make friends, took no pleasure in life but I worked on to make my parents believe that I could be a baker. After several years I had mastered the habits and skills of my father. He was proud and happy, for he had a descendant in his trade. My mother sensed my unhappiness, the death of my spirit, but she was compelled to abide by the decision of her husband. I loved my mother and respected my father, and I still hoped for some change in my life. After three years of apprenticeship I passed the examination and was now a baker.

My parents built a new bakeshop, larger, more modern. Soon after this, a national calamity befell Germany when Hitler took over the government. Most of the boys of my age joined the Nazi party. I had always been a private citizen—an individualist—and had no wish to wear a uniform of any kind. My mother felt as I did about this new life that was being forced on the nation, but my father insisted that we must join the party in the interests of our business. I could not understand this. Why must a businessman join the party to keep his business? I asked myself. Some years later my father was elected a deputy of the treasury department, then the leader of the bakers, then chairman of some banks, finally leader of all trades in the county. I thought my father was a man obsessed with obtaining such honors as might be bestowed upon him. It was not until much later that I realized what my father was doing.

My mother and I hated the party, because my father was seldom at home, leaving us to care for the business ourselves. Nobody knew what this party was up to. Very often my parents exchanged hard words as they argued over its purposes, something that had never happened before. My father gave his life for the party, to make good for my mother and me. We never joined the party or any organization affiliated with it.

In the meantime I worked hard in the bakeshop, and after five more years I passed the final examination as a master baker. Now my parents' wishes had been fulfilled. Nobody asked me if I was happy, but I am sure my mother sensed the conflict inside me. It was during this time that I discovered what a great burden a person can carry if he has the will power and faith in God, to the ultimate gain of his self-confidence and character.

My confidence and faith in God were put to the supreme test when I received the order to join the army. The conflict I felt within myself seemed impossible of solution. I went to ask my father if he could defer my order, but he said he could not give preferential treatment even to his own son. I was thereupon conscripted into the army.

There are limits to what any man can endure. I prayed for strength to enable me to carry on. Many times I doubted the love and wisdom of God. My life seemed hard beyond belief, and I sought in vain for an explanation of the disappointments I had been called upon to endure. Disappointed from my first years of life, compelled to the renunciation of my own wishes, pressed into service in a uniform I hated, life seemed very cruel indeed.

But my prayers were granted, and from some source I found the strength to continue. My heart was heavy, but I left our home to join the army.

A new chapter of life began for me, far from home, among strange men with different habits and ways of life. Though each soldier was an individual in his own right, this individuality appeared to be lost within the smothering confines of the army. The uniform seemed to strip us of our very souls. I had a very unpleasant time, more so, perhaps, because I experienced difficulty in adjusting to the loss of identity. I was compelled to call upon all of my strength of character in living up to army regulations, and everyone told me that I was a good soldier. Many times I felt like weeping, not because I considered myself too good for military service or felt that I should be an exception, but because I felt the wrongness of what I was doing. It is possible too that I suffered from a feeling of insecurity, and that, after so many disappointments, I found it hard to take orders from somebody whom I knew to be less well educated than myself. Still, I had the desire to be a good soldier, carried out my duties, and was clean and neat. No one could accuse me of shirking my responsibilities.

My order called for a three-months' exercise, which time would soon be over, for which I was very glad. However, on the morning of September 1, 1939, we were ordered into the barracks yard to hear the bad news: Germany had declared war on Poland. All my hopes of going home vanished into thin air. Every one of us was asking the same question: Why and how could this happen to us?

Once the news was transmitted a busy schedule began for every unit. Some of us were ordered to be transferred to the infantry, some to the navy or marines. I went immediately to the commander and asked permission to join the medical staff. My papers, education, and records showed that I was qualified, and two weeks later I was on my way to join an army medical school. I was happy, for now I could realize my own desire to be a doctor, and perhaps, by the time I had completed my medical education, the war would be over.

The doctors, astonished at my knowledge and handling of medical matters, gave me more and greater responsibilities, and I took it very seriously, giving my heart and soul to this profession of my choice; nothing was too hard for me. In my letters to my parents I described my satisfaction with my new duties. My mother, reading between the lines, was sorrier than ever that she had been unable to further my desire to be a doctor, but she had been powerless to alter the decision of her husband.

While at the time I had not understood my father's pride in his own trade, thinking him selfish, in later years I came to understand his wish to preserve the family tradition; he had, I realized, worked very hard to establish and keep his name, and he had stood in the foreground in the Nazi party to save our family and the business which I would carry on. I was like a straw in the wind, dreaming of success in my chosen profession, yet having to follow the course my father had charted for me.

A year passed, and I was still in medical training. My ambition and adherence to duty had resulted in my being promoted to corporal in the medical staff and in being granted a fourteen-day leave. I drove home, overjoyed to see my parents, my sister, and my friends. Those fourteen days passed swiftly, but I enjoyed each one to the fullest, describing in great detail my life in the medical school, proud of my success and forgetting the shadow of disappointment which had darkened my previous life. I rested from the hard work in the hospital, saving my strength for the future. No one could know then what the future held in store. For my part, I made no effort to see too far into the future, living in the present only.

My father's work with the party kept him very busy, and I saw him only at night, but he was even prouder of my protion than I was. My leave was over all too soon, and I went back to school, little knowing, as I bade my parents good-bye, that it was good-bye for a long time. Returning to my post,

I received order of transfer to the medical staff in a battalion of occupation troops in Holland. It was June, 1940, and the train, rolling west, stopped in several larger towns where more and more soldiers got on board. One evening in early July we arrived at our destination. Some troopers had made quarters in advance, and I found a very good furnished house as medical center. The next day the doctor came to take over as the leader of the medical staff. There were four men in the staff—the doctor, as officer, and three corporals.

Among the occupation troops there were no wounded, and we had only the usual illnesses to contend with. I had time to look around, enjoying my leisure-time strolls in the streets. I saw only the most favorable aspects of a strange country, ate in restaurants and browsed in libraries, met many Dutch people and made friends at once. I never bothered anybody, nor did anybody bother me. I knew I was an intruder, but I tried to be courteous and honest, and I felt that I had won the friendship of these people. I could go back to Holland at any time and find a cordial reception.

We stayed only a short time in this area, but one experience occurred which I will never forget. My medical leader, an officer, had wrecked his own car, and, since it took too long to repair it, he entered a private garage, took a car which belonged to a Hollander, and drove away. The Hollander reported this to the field police of the German Army, and the doctor was arrested and taken to jail. I never saw him again. I could not understand how it was possible for a German officer to steal a car; it was a terrible experience for me, and I was ashamed.

Soon after this incident our battalion left for France. In August we came to St. Lo in Normandy. St. Lo was an old town, and here too I made many friends. My knowledge of the French language made it easy for me to get along, and I found a very good quarter for our ambulance. The director of the Assurance Sociale gave me permission to take over the second flat in his building. As I came to ask him, I saw that he was a veteran of World War I, and I gave him the salute of honor and asked him politely. After this we became friends. Later on he invited me to dinner in his family home, and we had a very pleasant evening.

I had met many interesting people in these years, enjoyed my stay in their countries and made friends everywhere, but now I was anxious to go home. This, of course, was impossible, while the war still raged in Europe. I was afraid of what was coming, for, though I was safe in the army of occupation, there was no certainty that I would not be sent to the battle areas.

Another order came: Paris. I was happy to see Paris. Everything I had heard about Paris was beautiful—like the city itself. In my spare time I strolled down the Champs Elysées, Place de l'Opéra, visited St. Germain. I had time to visit the museums, churches, and galleries. I saw Montmartre, the Grave of the Unknown Soldier, Arc de Triomphe. There was much to be seen in this city of beauty, and I was eager to see more and more of the scenery of the surrounding countryside. I loved the French people and truly believed that they loved me. My mother's teaching about respecting my neighbor brought me the confidence and love of those to whom I applied it.

I spent almost two years in France. After leaving Paris I was stationed in Dijon, a very old and very beautiful town. Here too I found many friends whom I wished never to leave. The situation grew more serious when Germany declared war on Russia. All of us looked to the future with misgivings. I prayed that I might be spared actual combat; I was not a hero, and up until now I had neither seen nor heard a bullet. The future frightened me; every single day I was glad to be alive, and I prayed for an end to this war against which my nature rebelled. I had no idea how bad things were going to be. In my letters to my parents I made no effort to disguise my feeling about war, my native repugnance to the occupation. I was convinced that Germany could not win, and begged my parents many times to sell our property in East Prussia and to move to the western border of Germany. I do not know if they ever received these letters.

In April, 1942, I was ordered to the front. I traveled from Dijon to the place of appointment in middle Germany, but bypassed the garrison and went home to East Prussia. My parents were surprised to see me, having had no notice that I was coming. After being away for three years, three days were entirely insufficient in which to tell them about all my experiences and thoughts, and many things that I told had better been left unsaid; but my mother understood me perfectly. All too soon the three days were gone, and I bade my parents good-bye, knowing this time that it would be for a very long time, perhaps forever. As I hugged my mother I cried like a small boy, wondering if I would ever see her again. My mother's eyes were dry, but I know there were tears in her heart, for she must have known that this was good-bye forever. It was perhaps a blessing, at this time, that we could not see into the future.

I left my hometown alone, none of my family accompanying me to the station. My mind was filled with sadness, and I asked God for help and understanding of this situation. A fear of the unknown, as well as a fear of losing my parents, hung like a dark cloud over me. To my question—if the Lord had forgotten me or if I had forgotten the Lord—I could find no answer. My way was prescribed for me, and no alternate course was open to me.

Soon I came at the place of appointment, where I waited for further orders. After one week I was ordered to replace an ambulance attendant in the front lines deep in Russia. Until now I had no real conception of what war really means, and my heart was filled with fear and sadness, though outwardly I tried to be courageous, and nobody saw I was frightened of the coming days. Fourteen days took us to our destination, and they were fourteen days and fourteen nights of sorrow and fear. I was to be an ambulance attendant—a human being going into war to help others, going where people were killing each other. I often wondered whether this was kindness or cruelty.

My mind, wandering back to childhood, could not help but reflect how wonderful life had been during my school days, with all my friends about me, and with the love and companionship of my parents and sister. Who could say what life would be like after this terrible nonsensical war? I didn't know it, but I was now embarking on the cruelest period of my life.

On the night of the fourteenth day we came to our destination, perhaps ten miles behind our lines. As soon as the train stopped we had to get off at once; the Russians had learned about this transport and were firing upon it with long-range cannons. It was a harrowing experience. Under the cannonade we marched to our unit, a seemingly endless march. The entire horizon seemed to be aflame, the projectiles falling and exploding about us. The road was covered with dead horses, soldiers, and burning wagons and cars. We stumbled along, not knowing which one of us would be hit next. At dawn the next day I came to my unit, where I was to replace the ambulance attendant they had lost. My superior officer told me that we were now in the second line of fire, but that tomorrow we would have to relieve the front line and some casualties were expected. The relief was planned for noontime.

Between dawn and noon of that day I kept silent, talking

with my soul and praying to God to keep me strong and calm, also asking blessings for my parents. The hands of the clock kept moving, the strain on our nerves growing with each second. We all felt this, smoking one cigarette after another, waiting for the signal to relieve the front line. The order to form a lineup came like a fanfare, everyone putting out his cigarette, pulling on his helmet and getting ready to move. We had to cross an open field, though the Russian soldiers were on the other side upon a hill where they had a very good view of us, firing upon us as soon as we started to come out of our dugout. My job began right now: everywhere there was somebody hit who was crying for help.

I wanted to cry when I came to my first wounded soldier. One of his legs was torn off at the trunk. I knelt down and tried with shaking hands to give him first aid, put him in my tent-cloth and dragged him back to the medical tent. All around us the bombs and grenades shook the ground, but I made it to the tent with my wounded fellow man.

I was pale and scared when at last we reached safety. After a short prayer I went again to fulfil my mission. Late in the afternoon, crawling and running, we had reached the front line, but the loss of soldiers was enormous.

During the next few weeks we didn't leave our trench, for the Russians fought for every inch of ground they lost, many thousands of bullets and grenades being exchanged between both armies. We lost many soldiers, but replacements came every week. This position was held for almost four weeks; then the order came from army headquarters to take the position from the enemy. The attack was set for 4:00 A.M. the next day. Stukas and fighter planes came howling nearer, and at precisely 4:00 A.M. the bombs exploded in the Russian line. It sounded as if the earth were bursting. This offensive took the Russians by surprise, the survivors drawing back several miles. As soon as we had taken possession of their trenches we found that we had been fighting against women, for there were few men among the dead.

After this battle we advanced for perhaps one hundred miles without making contact with the enemy. It did not seem to occur to our leaders that the Russians were leading us into a trap. They let us penetrate deep into Russian territory, since the next Russian line was behind the river Don. We built our trench on the west side, facing the Russian soldiers on the east. Here too there were daily exchanges of bullets across the river.

The Russian Army leaders knew the wintertime to be their best ally, whereas the German leaders seemed to have learned nothing from the previous winter. The river Don, running from north to south as far as Stalingrad, was the natural defense line for the Russians. It was a severe test for our army, a nerve-racking encounter which may have been the turning point in World War II. My unit had to reinforce the efforts of the Sixth Army in and around Stalingrad, which had been the scene of violent action since November and would, presumably, soon be encircled. It was our job to keep open the northwest side for reinforcements and to bring out the sick and wounded. We moved as fast as was possible in the bitter cold and deep snow. In the first days of December we came to Kalatch, the last town before Stalingrad and virtually a suburb of that city, where we had to fight for every inch of our advance. We kept fighting for the next fourteen days, not knowing that it was we ourselves who were encircled.

This circle in Stalingrad was a hell on earth, each house a battlefield. It was here that my luck ran out, though I didn't know at the time which would be better—to be dead or taken prisoner of war. On Sunday morning, December 20, I was captured by some Russian soldiers, though the Red Cross band around my left arm was clearly visible. To be a prisoner of war, especially in the most violent battle of that war, seemed to be ill fortune almost beyond enduring. I felt that I would be better off dead. As soon as the soldiers had taken our private property—rings, watches, warm clothes, and boots —they brought us back to the commander, who was a commissar of the NKVD. He was quartered in an old shack; it was here that my mistreatment began. As soon as he saw me he took up his whip and beat my face till it bled. I was, of course, an intruder on his soil, but I was also a prisoner of war without weapons, besides being an ambulance attendant entitled to protection under the rules of the Geneva Convention. Such cruelty seemed unbelievable in the twentieth century, but it was only a foretaste of what was to come. I wished with all my heart that I could die.

We were kept in this shack until all fifteen prisoners had made their statements about name, rank, and unit. In the meantime one prisoner asked to go to the toilet, one guard accompanying him. They were scarcely out of sight when we heard a shot, and the guard came back alone. In my heart I envied the dead man, for there was no way of knowing what would happen to us.

We were asked questions about the strength of our unit, but since we were cut off from our unit we were unable to answer—and even if we had known we would not have told them. After this interrogation we were forced to march about ten miles, and from that point on we had to shovel snow to clear the road so the cars could pass and bring food and reinforcements to Stalingrad. It was bitterly cold, and we were made to work from dawn till late at night. The guards brought our food along, which consisted of two pieces of table sugar, one-half salt herring, and one piece of dry black bread, the daily ration for each man. There was nothing to drink, so we ate snow.

At night, when the moon was shining, the guards came

and drove us back in our shelter, a two-room house, unoccupied now in wartime, which was located on the outskirts of a small village. The former inhabitants of this house had taken the windows, furniture, and everything movable. It was cold and drafty, the wind blowing snow in the open windows as we sat on the floor close to one another to keep warm, shivering and freezing and waiting for the next morning when we would go again out in the desert of snow. The guards came very early in the morning, when it was still dark, and we had to report the number of our crew before we received our breakfast, which consisted of one cup of hot water and one slice of dry, black rye bread (suchari). After breakfast we were counted again before being sent out in the bitter cold. In this manner fourteen days passed. Each one of us came down with some form of sickness, several beginning to swell in the face and legs, others suffering the first symptoms of pneumonia. Backache was a common ailment. I told the guard that we needed a doctor, but he didn't understand what I was talking about.

Some days later I became sick and couldn't go to work any more. I was burning with fever. When it became apparent to the guard that we were little more than walking corpses, he promised to call a doctor. He let us stay in our shelter till the doctor came and examined us. The doctor, seeing at first glance that there was nothing he could do, granted permission to bring all fifteen men into a hospital. We were all sick and burning with fever, but we had to wait till a truck came. We had no appetite for food, but we craved water.

The truck came the next day. Two guards helped us to board the truck, giving us two loaves of bread and some sugar for all of us; then we started to drive across country. We didn't know in what direction we were traveling, but we heard the artillery fire from the front, or thought we did.

37

Though sometimes it seemed that our minds were already suffering from delusion.

Two days later the truck stopped at a train station, and we were transferred to the freight wagon of a train. After two days of riding on the train we came to the town of Volsk, located south of Gorki, which was our destination. As soon as we appeared marching in the streets, the people of this town threw stones and everything they could find at us, swearing hysterically and spitting at us, calling us fascists and imperialists. I understood the source of this hatred, for we were intruders on Russian soil, but we were now prisoners of war, without weapons, sick and in need of understanding, and it seemed odd to me that they did not realize that few of us would have gone voluntarily to war, especially against Russia.

Soon we arrived at the hospital, a big stone house, formerly a school, but now in wartime, housing the wounded and sick prisoners. As we reached the entrance we found the air so full of stench and decay that we could scarcely breathe. Brutish sounds came from within, and I knew that inside was a human being at his last breath. Lord God, bless us and keep us, I thought, little realizing that I was on the threshold of my most horrible experience in life.

We entered the so-called office, where we were registered and compelled to take off all our clothing and put it in bags. These would be given back to us when we were healthy again. We were provided with a pair of drawers, a shirt, a blanket, and slippers, and, thus thinly clothed, sent to the bathhouse, some fifty yards away in the backyard, to take a bath. On the way to the bathhouse two of the fifteen collapsed and died, their hearts unable to endure this sudden change of temperature. We were given a bowl with hardly one gallon of water in it for our bath; then we marched back to the main building to find a bed.

What I had seen in the first hour was enough to convince

me that we would be fortunate if any of us survived this ordeal. Pitiful specimens of humanity, walking human bodies like skeletons, their heads bald, their eyes sunken, walking with hands on the wall to support themselves, were crying for help, praying for redemption. The room in which I was placed was the isolation room, filled with those patients who were deathly ill. Here two bedsteads were put together, with boards across them on which five men could lie. I had to lie between four men who were sick with dysentery and typhus. We had only two pillows and one blanket for the five of us. Besides this bed there were five others. A bucket in one corner served as a chamberpot, but few of these men were well enough to reach the chamberpot in time, relieving themselves on the floor or wherever they happened to be. The stench was terrible, not only in this room but in all parts of the hospital, for the only lavatory was in the basement. We had no towels or anything with which to clean our hands. In the morning, when the first "nurse" came on duty, she asked, "How many are dead?" After we gave her the number, she asked, "What, no more?"

The dead bodies were taken out of the beds, undressed, and taken away. The same woman who had done the undressing brought out bread. We could not eat, putting the bread under our pillows against the time when we would be hungry, though many times the bread was taken away from us. In this way the disease spread from one room to another, and the entire house was soon an island of dying souls. When I entered this hospital the number of occupants had been close to three thousand, all the rooms being crowded to the fullest capacity. The mortality rate in the months from January to August was exactly 80 per cent. During my first fourteen days I was sick with typhus and had an average temperature of 102 degrees. I couldn't eat a bite, but I badly wanted something to drink.

Every morning my nearest neighbor in the bed was dead. Often I envied these dead men, but when I saw how a dead body was treated—how they grasped it by the feet and dragged it out of the bed, the head striking the floor, my will to live was rekindled, and I hoped and prayed that I would get well and be permitted to leave this terrible house.

Most of the prisoners had typhus exanthematous, a deadly disease which requires special care, but here there was a shortage of doctors and drugs. I do not believe that anyone made a serious effort to save or cure a prisoner. The registration of the dead prisoners was simple, the nurse writing the name of the deceased on a strip of newspaper with a pencil and fastening this on the wrist with a cord or bandage. Nobody knows where these creatures are buried.

In the latter part of January my temperature dropped to normal, but my body was as emaciated as the others, my weight having dropped to ninety-six pounds. My strength had deserted me, and I was walking like all the others, keeping my hands on the wall for support. It took me almost four more weeks to be able to walk alone without any support.

Since I was a medical student, I was compelled to work in this hospital, and I was appalled at the manner in which the ill and wounded were treated. No care was exercised for the wounded, the bandages being taken off, laundered, and, after drying, put on again without being sterilized. All of the injured soldiers had worms in their wounds. It was shocking to witness their suffering. Besides those who were wounded, there were many hundreds with frostbitten hands and feet, most of them frozen in the third degree, which means that the frozen part of the hand or foot had already turned black. Though I barely had the strength to hold myself upright, I tried to help these men as best I could.

During the afternoon hours I went through all the rooms

to see if I could help someone. I had no drugs or medical help, but I had the knowledge and ability to make a diagnosis and could suggest what should be done and give the order to the nurse. Starvation, shortage of drugs, and carelessness accounted for many deaths.

I was in this hospital almost eight months, sickened by the incredible disregard for the welfare of human beings. A commission was expected to arrive from Moscow to inspect the hospital, so a housecleaning was arranged, some women from out of town brought in to wash the windows. We had to scrub the floors ourselves. The nurses made some tablecloths from cotton, and for the first time they gave us sheets and pillowcases. The commission went through all the rooms except the isolation room. The convalescent prisoners were outside in the garden, taking a sunbath and waiting for the commission; our instructions were to tell them how grateful we were for being helped in our sickness. Nobody expected the commission to ask why so many prisoners had died, and none of the others had the courage to answer. I, being a member of the Red Cross, felt a certain compulsion to answer this question, and I told them everything I had seen in the eight months I had been there, concluding with the statement that, if I were ever granted my freedom, I would tell the Red Cross how the U.S.S.R. treated the members of the Red Cross and sick human beings. After the commission left I was declared healthy enough to go to work in a labor camp which was connected with a cement factory. My weight was still ninety-six pounds, and my strength seemed to have left me utterly.

I had never known that a human being could endure such misery, and I hoped and prayed to stay alive and to return to my parents and sister. Here in my lonely captivity deep in Russia, behind well-guarded fences, I realized for the first time how much I loved and missed my family. Often I thought of the bakeshop, wishing that I could eat all the leftovers and

41

the flour which was spilled on the floor. Hunger makes animals of human beings, and the Russians took advantage of this knowledge by offering us two ounces more of bread each day, for which we would work doubly hard. The work in this cement factory was manual, since the factory itself had been established almost fifty years earlier, using old-fashioned methods and manned by political or criminal prisoners before we prisoners of war came.

At the railroad station, where the cement came in freight wagons, I had to unload the cement, shovel fifty pounds in paper bags, and carry it on my back into a storeroom. We were dusty from head to toe, the dust so thick in our ears and nose when the wind was blowing that we could scarcely breathe, but it was necessary to unload the wagon if we wanted to get our extra two ounces of bread that evening. Returning to the barracks at night, we seldom found water to clean our faces and hands, which contributed to our low spirits by forcing us to go about dusty and pale, looking like walking corpses. Counting the days and hoping for the end of the war was all that kept us going. It was now 1943, and none of us could or would believe that we would be here for several more years.

In this factory a Jewish woman doctor was in charge of the prisoners. This doctor knew that I was suffering from poor health and found time to talk to me as I came in the ambulance for treatment, questioning me about my descent, my education, and my family. I knew that I had found a friend, and she promised to help me, but she told me that she could do no more than was possible for her as a Russian citizen. I understood her position very well and didn't ask for anything that could get her in trouble. She told me that she would grant permission for the most seriously ill prisoners to transfer to another camp. When we reported to the ambulance for physical examination, several days later, I praised the Lord when I found that I was among the twenty-five sick men to be transferred, and my gratitude to this doctor was unbounded. Still, there was no way of knowing whether the new camp would be better or worse. We had hoped before to leave the worse for a better, but each time our hopes had been dashed and we had found ourselves in a worse environment than that which we had left.

I was one of fifty eventually transferred to Susdal, a small town with a monastery several hundred years old. Its beautiful architecture was in evidence, but since the Revolution it had become dilapidated, uncared for by the present custodians, the buildings now housing the officers of the captured army. This camp was what was called a transit camp. The NKVD, or state police, checked the records of each prisoner from the day he had been captured. If contradictory statements were issued, or doubtful information given, those persons were questioned again and again. I found in this camp higher officers with some scientific background. One of them was the world-famed discoverer of Targesin, and was questioned many times a day before finally being transferred to an unknown location.

It was bitterly cold, with much snow on the ground, when we left Susdal, our destination unknown. The train was headed east. None of us knew what fate had in store for us, though we were still hoping to find a place where conditions would be a little better and where we could perhaps stay until the end of the war, at which time we hoped to be permitted to go home to our families. Home seemed more real to me than during the time I had actually been there. How I would love my family, keep my parents, and help them in their old age! I would do everything—if only I could find them alive. My thoughts were interrupted as the train stopped and we were forced to get off. It was night time, and as soon as we left the train were were counted by the guards, then told the bad news: our destination was Yelabuga, almost thirty miles distant, and we would have to march. It was near to forty degrees below zero, with five feet of snow; we were hungry and thirsty, and so tired that we had could have fallen down and slept. Many of us collapsed, getting up and moving again after a short rest on the ground, and some could not get up at all. We tried very hard to bring each one to his feet again, taking hold of his arm and carrying him so that we would not lose anybody. During the last few miles of our march we saw houses on the horizon, only to find that they were mirages of our exhausted minds. Three miles from Yelabuga I collapsed and felt myself powerless to rise. It was an odd feeling, strangely comfortable, and I wished very much to die. Death due to exposure to cold would appear to be easy to endure. The commandant of Camp Yelabuga knew we were coming and had sent a sleigh to bring the most helpless. I was put in the sleigh along with several others, and after an hour's ride we arrived at Camp Yelabuga.

As soon as the sleigh arrived at camp, the doctor came to see us. They gave us hot tea and a slice of bread, but I was unable to eat or drink, and the doctor, who was a woman, paid more attention to me. She realized immediately that I was in serious condition and gave me an injection. My surroundings were obliterated as I lay in a pool of darkness and rest. In my drugged state of mind, I thought I saw my mother and sister and talked with them. My heart and soul were always at home.

After a few days I found myself back again in a so-called isolation room. It took me almost three weeks to get on my feet, but I had to stay in the sickroom four more weeks. Upon my release from the sickroom, I realized my new place of confinement was not a bit better than the places where I had previously been held captive. Camp Yelabuga had been the residence of some priests in the era of the czars. Here too the beautiful buildings were in a state of decay. The church was used as a storage house for food and empty boxes, the main building housing more of the prisoners. Plank beds had been built in the rooms, each person having a space of about thirty-five inches. Fifteen hundred men were in this camp, sixty being confined in one room.

In January, 1944, the commandant of this camp issued a bulletin to the effect that the camp had to manage itself. This meant that we had to carry our own wood for the bakeshop, kitchen, laundry, etc., keep the water pumps in working condition, man the electric station and provide all necessities for our daily life. Under the supervision of a captured German officer, who was called the camp-leader, different labor groups were set up, some working in the kitchen, others in the bakeshop, in the laundry, on the water pumps, electric station, and ambulance. All of these groups found the work difficult, but the hardest work was carrying the wood for the entire camp. Early in the morning this group marched out, coming back at night with the wagon loaded with wood. They had to pull the wagon themselves, since no horses were provided, and in wintertime sleighs were used in place of the wagon. For this work in the wood brigade the men got four ounces more of bread and a thicker soup, extra food coming from the rations of the other men, rather than from an increase in food delivered to the camp. The result was that the soup for the rest of us was much more watery that it had been. All of us tried very hard to go only once with the wood brigade, in order that the thicker soup might be evenly apportioned among us all. The strain to our bodies meant nothing to us: it was important only that we fill up once in a while.

In the meantime America had made an agreement with Russia to help the Russian population and the prisoners of war. When the provisions of this pact began to be carried out, we felt a little more secure; more drugs were available and the mortality rate dropped, due in part to the fact that the prisoners were becoming better adjusted to this kind of life. The daily ration was still the same, but at least we could count on getting it, which had not always been the case heretofore. Each prisoner was given a daily minimum of six hundred grams of dark rye bread, which contained 60 per cent water, ten grams of flour or peas or potatoes, ten grams of oil or fish, and ten grams of sugar. In comparison, one ounce is equivalent to twenty-eight grams. I had been in Yelabuga almost three years, but it was still only 1944, and every day and month seemed an eternity. Most nerve-racking of all, we had to listen to the news over the radio; the polit commissar turned on the radio so that we could hear how the Russian Army was repelling the German Army and that Germany would soon be the battlefield. We still had hopes that the war would be over soon and that we could go home. In December, 1944, German towns were mentioned for the first time in the news, and we sat listening while our hopes of ever seeing our relatives again died within us. We were still thousands of miles away from home in 1945, and the Russian Army was in Germany, with thousands of people fleeing from East Prussia while we remained captive in Russia, starving and waiting to return to our homes. Our thoughts on New Year's Eve, 1944, were of home, and we were praying and hoping for a happy 1945.

In February, 1945, the name of my hometown was mentioned in the news; the town, according to the newscast, was virtually razed after a fierce battle. I sat on my bed and cried, feeling an emptiness inside me and knowing that I would never see my parents again. But my faith was stronger than my emotions, and I persisted in the hope that there would someday be a reunion of all of us. After all these years in prison we found ourselves unable to believe one word the Russians were saying. Our only hope—that America and the free world would ask for release of all prisoners of war—gave us the courage to remain alive. The end of the war, in May, 1945, was a relief for all people on earth. The Russians devoted eight days to celebrating their victory over Nazi Germany. We prisoners thanked the Lord that we were alive, skeletons though we were, hoping still for the chance to return someday and build a new life. Would this be soon, we wondered—or how much longer would we have to stay? Could we carry on much longer under these terrible circumstances?

Several months after the end of the war the Russians brought trainload after trainload of furniture, food, clothing and equipment from Germany: they called this action "reparations." We saw Russian women dressed in the uniforms of Nazi officers, the stars and medals still on, obviously enjoying what they considered an attractive style. We found the spectacle ludicrous. As we marched our daily route to work, we found that the train station was loaded with all the furniture from Germany, now the property of the State, which made no effort to divide it among the people, leaving it at the mercy of the elements.

The Russian officials declared that we were no longer prisoners of war, giving us instead the title of "reparation workmen." There did not seem to be a great deal of difference. We lost all hope for our return to Germany. Nobody in the world could enforce our return. Most of the prisoners had died, no records kept of their passing, and now we were reparation workmen. The free world could only conjecture as to how many men had been captured and how many remained alive.

At Christmas, 1945, each one of us was permitted to send a postcard home. It was a propaganda move only, designed to show that Russia made no secret of its captured soldiers. We tried to contact our relatives, but nobody knew where they were living now. I wrote every month to my parents, but never received an answer, nor was my card returned. Few among us had made contact with our families, and most had abandoned hope of a reunion. Somehow I could not relinquish the hope. Perhaps I will find them when I get back, I comforted myself—but when will it be? One year had passed since the end of the war, and our lives had not changed for the better.

In August, 1946, there was great excitement in camp. Russia had decided to send home the first prisoners. We wondered who would be among them—the sick, the dystrophic, the older men? It was a question for which we found no answer. Nobody had any idea as to how the selection was to be made, but everyone of us had hopes of being chosen. The list, when it was made public, sealed our disappointment, for only fifty men were being sent home, and those fifty were so ill as to be nearly dead. However, the mere fact that any were being sent was reassuring; surely Russia had to release more of us. Then the free world and the government of Germany would learn about the numerous prisoners still alive in Russia and would claim their return. Unbreakable faith in the humanity of the free world gave us the strength to carry on and the will power to live.

Soon after this another transport was planned, and I was among the three hundred men selected. We were issued new clothes and fed well for almost fourteen days, happily waiting for the time to come when we would march to the train station. It seemed certain that the new clothes had been given us to make a good impression on our return to freedom, but after six days of riding in the train we stopped at Selonodolsk on the river Volga, our destination. The guard told us that we had to do reparation work for at least two more years. It seemed the final blow to our spirits, which now lapsed to a point of hopeless acceptance of the inevitable.

From now on we were on our own. The cost of our living was set at five hundred rubles a month for each of us, and we had to work very hard to meet our expenses, since there were some fifty men working inside the camp whom we were compelled to support. We alternated between two factories, one a paper mill and the other a wartime ammunition plant which was now producing aluminum. Our daily fixed quota was so extremely high that we could never fulfill it. I worked for some time in the paper mill, then inside the camp and, in the wintertime, on the river Volga, which was the hardest job. We had to break open the ice upon the river and fish out the logs which were floated in the summer but which were now frozen, pulling them out with long chains. Cold and wet, our clothes frozen to our bodies, we had to work doubly hard in order to keep warm. Many of us suffered frostbitten noses and ears, our hands and feet numbed by the intense cold.

While I was working in the paper mill I made friends with some Russian civilians, asking them about their way of life and how they felt about the Communist party. They would talk to me only when we were alone, fearing to be overheard by the Communists. I discovered that the Russian people were waiting for something to free them, but it would have to come from outside. I consider this to be true even today, regardless of the statements coming out of Russia. State-owned co-operatives (Kolkhozes) are not satisfying the people. The politburo has trained the people to work as industriously as if each individual was an owner, but personal interest in one's work is entirely lacking. The rule is: He who is not working shall not eat; therefore, every human being must work regardless of what kind of work he does.

The same applies to family life: children of a certain

age have to join the youth movement, and are taken away from their parents, to be trained in the communistic ideology and in the profession which seems most vital to the welfare of the nation. A citizen who makes the mistakes of talking against the Communists is tried before a political justice as a criminal against the security of the State and sentenced to hard labor far away from home, his partner in marriage deported in the opposite direction. There is no opportunity for such a family to be reunited, and the marriage is therefore annulled. Such is life under communism. I was born and raised in a good Christian family, where I learned about capitalism, democracy, and national socialism, and now, in Russia, I was living under the Communist system. I went through this "paradise for laborers" with open eyes, but I was unable to find one respect in which the system was not repugnant to freedom-loving people. Nobody owned private property; even radios were to be found only in the office of the political instructor, who listened only to what he was permitted to hear. In the apartments were loud-speakers, through which the occupants could listen only to what the instructor had tuned in. Cars and all other practical equipment were the property of the State. People in certain positions were permitted to make use of these cars, but nobody owned them. Who takes care of something that is not his own?

Farms and vital factories are the property of the State, all such institutions compelled to produce a quota which is fixed by the Department of Agriculture. The supervisors of these farms and factories are Communists, who shift the workers at will, to the places where they are most needed. If all the farms in one state produce only wheat, and all the farms in another state grow only potatoes, they still cannot exchange their product without permission from the authorities.

One incident which astonished me is indicative of the

manner in which these people are treated. We were working on a new road and couldn't fulfill our quota by a fixed date. One day before this date there appeared a truck filled with cleanly dressed women from the next town to lay the asphalt on the new road. I asked several women, "Why do you come here to work with asphalt in your good clothes?" The answer was shocking to me: the women had been in town, waiting in line for their groceries, when the police came and picked up all women on the street and brought them here to work. Their responsibilities as wives and mothers were of no concern to anybody; what was important was that the street be finished on time. Such incidents made me more determined than ever to keep alive the hope of returning to my own country, though when it would be was a question we could not answer.

I had to work in turns in the paper mill, in the aluminum factory, and on the Volga. We could thank the Lord for the fact that the time goes quickly even during periods when it seems that the food shortage will kill you. For two years we worked as hard as our physical constitutions would permit, never once reaching the prescribed quota. In mid-1947 about 50 men—those with some injuries and frostbitten limbs —were selected to be transported home. We were happy for them, because their lives were in danger under the conditions prevailing in Russia, but whether they reached their native country nobody knows.

After their departure only 250 men remained in camp. We did not know what fate had in store for us, though all of us hoped to be released some day. Near the end of 1947 there was much excitement in camp when somebody learned that our camp would be abandoned soon because we could not meet our expenses. We did believe that we would be repatriated now, but it proved to be only a rumor. Week after week passed with no break in our routine. One day in November we were not made to go to work; the fence was locked, and we were assembled to hear the news from the camp officer, who told us that we could not make as much money as was needed and that therefore this camp would be closed down within a week. He did not tell us what our own fate was to be, but we were issued clean uniforms, boots, and coats which came from the Russian Army, and fed well for almost fourteen days, which we took as a sure sign of impending repatriation. On the last day we marched smiling to the train station, entered the coach, and made ourselves as comfortable as possible, closing the doors and starting a fire in the stoves which were in the middle of each car. Late at night, when the train started to pull out, we were tired from excitement, and every one of us fell asleep. While we could not keep track of the direction in which we were heading, we did not doubt that we were going home. After the fourth day we planned to watch for the names of towns we were passing through, placing one man at a very small window. In the morning of the sixth day he turned from the window, frightened, to tell that we were heading east and right now were crossing the European-Asian border. We could not believe him, rushing to the window to see for ourselves.

It was true; we were going east. Where would be our destination? we asked ourselves. Were we to be made to endure another period of hardship? Lord help us, we thought. Disappointed from many years of captivity, undernourished and ill, it did not seem possible that we could endure further deprivation of a normal life. Five years had passed since I was captured, with no word from my parents and no sign of release. My will to live very nearly left me. My faith and hope wavered as I asked myself whether I could any longer believe in God. My spirit was assailed with doubt, but after a night of silent prayers I was filled with renewed faith. I had to be patient and to believe. I was still alive, and the chance of being released was always present. I strove to fight down my doubts, though I often wondered whether it would not be better if I were dead, for who knew what I would find when I returned to my country, whether I would find my relatives and under what conditions?

Several more days passed before we could see where we were landing: Karpinsk, south of Sverdlovsk in the Ural Mountains. This would be our place to live or to die. The camp itself was bigger than any we had ever seen before. We wondered how many prisoners were here, and whether we would have a chance to be released soon. The more prisoners who were waiting for their return, the smaller our chances would be. To our surprise we found about eighteen hundred men at camp, and our coming brought the total to about two thousand.

As soon as we entered Camp Karpinsk we had to pass all the usual examination and registration. It was a full day before we were divided and placed to our brigades. I found myself in a brigade selected to work in the quarry. It was our job to move the railroad tracks. Every morning when we came to work, a Russian foreman was there handing out shovels, pickaxes, jimmies and jacks; then he gave his instructions to the leader of our brigade. He blew a whistle, at which signal we took up our tools and started our march to the place where we would work, two miles or more from the toolroom. We began work immediately upon arrival, leveling the ground for the new tracks, removing the old tracks from their ties, carrying the tracks on our shoulders as far as one hundred feet, while others dug out the ties preparatory to moving them to the new locatioin. The ties were of oak, weighing up to two hundred pounds, and each tie was carried by two men. Another group had to place the ties, lay and nail down the tracks, level the tracks, and tighten the ties. It was very hard work, especially in winter, we never came close to fulfilling our quota.

We had to work in temperature of thirty-five degrees below zero, and in a section of country which has almost five months of winter. The clothing was entirely inadequate. Many times, when our clothes were wet, we had to dry them inside the barracks. Boots and gloves were of different sizes, and we were forced to exchange them among ourselves in order to achieve a proper fit. Somehow we got through 1948, though we did not count days, months, or years any more. Every morning was a new day, and as long as we were alive we hoped for something unexpected, for some help from the free world. Perhaps America and the Western powers would claim our release, we thought. We knew that the Russians did not care about the opinions of the free world but it was our only hope.

The Russians kept every move a secret, so that no one knew what was going on. They spread some rumors to keep us going, hoping, working. In the spring of 1949 another group was selected to be repatriated. This time only those who would go to East Germany and work there were chosen. Since I had been born in East Prussia, I was on the list to go home. As soon as I entered the ambulance for physical examination, the officer of the state police whispered to the doctor that he believed I was one of Hitler's SS men, judging by my height and looks. I did not pass the examination, and was forced to return to work. I was bitterly disappointed, having been so near to release, but after a few days I was myself again, hoping for better luck next time. The very same thing happened three times more, and when I was again summoned for the release examination, in October, 1949, I had little hope that I would be chosen. This time, however, my luck seemed to hold; another police officer was on duty, and gave his O.K. for my release. The date for our repatriation was set for November 3, 1949. Excitement was great, for this transport was the fifth to be released, and the departure of this group would leave only five hundred men at Karpinsk. We received new uniforms while waiting for the deadline. The train had been delayed by the deep snow, and, as day after day passed with no word of it, we began to believe that our repatriation was another false alarm. Three more days dragged by in fear, hope, and sorrow, each day seeming to be an eternity. Finally, on November 6, the train arrived, and we breathed freely again. Praise the Lord, we thought, we are finally going home.

As soon as the news was out, we dressed at once and went to the fence. Once more we had to stay in line and wait until our names were called to leave the camp. Outside the fence we had to form groups and wait until the last one had left the camp. One of the Russian officers gave the order, and we marched in silence to the train station, our minds occupied with the future. Each man's face mirrored his emotion: some were praying, some smiling happily, some fearful as they wondered what they would find at home.

Home. I could not go home, because my hometown was in Russian territory. Where shall I go to look for my relatives? I wondered. But my happiness at leaving this hell on earth was sufficient for the time being, and I knew I would find the strength to look around when I got there.

After an hour's march we came to the train station; surprisingly, our train was there and waiting. We were counted again, the officer in charge calling the name of each one who was permitted to enter the wagon. This procedure took almost the entire day. Late at night the train pulled out, and we knew we were going home at last. Joy and happiness filled our hearts for the first time in seven years; forgotten were the hardships, fear, and hunger. Thankful for survival, everyone prayed silently and fell asleep smiling happily.

When we awoke next morning, we found that the train was still rolling. This was a surprise, for usually when we rode a train they stopped at night. Our first stop was at noon, at which time they gave us our meal. The soup tasted delicious to us in this cold weather—for we were going home. Besides the soup we were given some bread. As soon as we had finished eating, the engineer blew the whistle and the train began to roll again. We spent twelve days on the train before reaching the Russian-Polish border, where the doors were locked and the guards took turns watching the train and the prisoners. We did not know the reason; some law, we supposed. Next morning we stopped at Brest Litovsk and had to leave our train, for the Polish government took over our transport through Poland. At Brest Litovsk, which is the transit station, the tracks are of a different width; therefore, the Russian trains cannot pass through Polish country. After we had left the train we saw that we were in some kind of camp again. In this camp one of our number called for a meeting, at which he read a resolution drawn up by the Anti-Fa. It was a "thank-you" note to Russia for the opportunity to work for Russia and for having been liberated from the Nazi regime; for being still alive and able to work in the future for the interests of the Communist party. Everyone was asked to sign this resolution. I could not and would not sign, discovering later that only a few had signed this statement. After this meeting the Polish government took charge of the whole affair, reading each prisoner's name, which was then repeated by the prisoner, along with his surname and date of birth, before he could enter the train on the opposite track. After several hours, when the examination was finished, about twenty-five men still remained outside. We did not know what had happened to them, but later we heard that they were wanted for some reason by the Polish government. Our nerves were on edge, tension and fear mixed with our hope. How long, we wondered, would it be till we were free? Hysterical laughter, jokes, and some talk about food could be heard among the crowd. In the eyes of most could be seen fear for the future. Many of us sat silently in a corner, praying for strength. The strain on men who had been so long in prison was almost unbearable.

The train headed west, destination Frankfort on the Oder, through the formerly German territory of East Prussia and the Corridor, through towns which had once been German territory, now occupied by Poland. What we saw in this part of the country was shocking: towns and villages abandoned, no signs of life at all, weed-grown streets, houses destroyed by war or exposed to the mercy of the elements and the ravages of decay. Some towns, heavily populated before the war, were now occupied by the Polish, with only a few Germans among them. A few of the remaining Germans came to the train station to beg for bread. We did not have much food for ourselves, but we gave them all we had left. They told us their war experiences and begged us to take them with us. We could not do a thing to help them. In my mind I visualized my parents in the same situation; I could think of nothing more terrible in life than to find my parents begging for bread. My fear grew within me, as I wondered where I should look for my parents and sister. Perhaps they had had the chance to flee East Prussia and save their lives. It was the only hope I had. The ride through this familiar part of my country was as endless as the worries and fear that beset my heart.

On the night of November 20 we arrived at Frankfort on the Oder. As soon as we left the train we were divided into two groups: those who were going to the East zone could board a train the same night, but those going to West Ger-

57

many had to spend the night in the waiting room and take the train the next morning. At 4:00 A.M. the train pulled out of Frankfort in the direction of Helmstedt, the end station of East Germany, arriving about 10:00 A.M. Across from Helmstedt is Friedland—the door to freedom, and the fulfilment of our hopes and dreams. On the other side, some two hundred yards away, we could see the Red Cross wagon, the American officers, the Salvation Army building, and the buses. Marching in groups of five, we passed the Russian guard at the border showed our discharge papers—and then were free.

As soon as we passed the guard we knelt to touch the ground. The American officers and Red Cross workers gave us a hospitable welcome. Buses carried us to the transit camp in Friedland, where we had our first decent bath and were given new underwear, food, and a bed. In the meantime we were registered and subjected to physical examination.

I could not rest until I knew something about my relatives. I was looking for the Red Cross office, finding it in the main building, a well-equipped office with photos and addresses of people who were expecting somebody back from prison camp or from East Germany. I went to the window for refugees from East Prussia and gave my name, asking for my parents and sister. The lady on duty went through book after book to find the names I had given her. I was shaking, the sweat running down my face, my heartbeat so loud I was sure everyone could hear it. I could not believe what the lady was telling me, having to ask her again and again. But it had the ring of truth, and I stood helplessly while her words bored into my very soul. My father had passed away in November, 1944; my mother had been shot down by Russian soldiers in 1945; my sister and both of her children had been displaced to Siberia and died of starvation in 1946; a niece had been repatriated in April, 1949. Everything broke down inside me; all my hope, the strength to which I had clung in the past seven years, left me with this terrible news. I was a stranger in West Germany, with no friends, no relatives, and no home.

I tried to pull myself together, wondering what to do first. In Friedland I received forty marks, enough to rent a room. I found a furnished room, paying 12.50 marks a week in advance, which left me sufficient money for food.

In the weeks to come I was unable to work and received unemployment compensation of 17.50 marks a week, but the room rent took most of the money. For three months I was under a doctor's care, taking calcium shots three times a week, and without the money to eat properly. I decided to go on my own and look for a position, but I found little sympathy for a homeless refugee. As a repatriated former soldier I had to work for less money than others. I was glad to earn an honest living. As soon as I had become adjusted to normal living, I tried to find my niece; the Red Cross helped me to locate her. Though she was living far from me, I nevertheless took several days off from my work to see her, for I wanted to know the terrible truth about my mother's death. When I went to her apartment, her landlady told me that she was working and would not be back until afternoon. It was still early in the day, but I went to the train station and waited until she came.

As train after train arrived without her I became more nervous by the minute, my heart beating heavily and my palms damp with perspiration. Finally I saw her leave the train, and I moved back a few steps to let her pass the ticket window. When she was beside me, I called her name. She looked at me and fell crying into my arms. I tried to calm her, but I was more nervous than she. With my last pennies we went into the nearest coffee house where we would be undisturbed.

She told me about the death of my father and the terrible death of my mother. She went on and on, telling me all her experiences during the time when the Russian soldiers had opened fire on my hometown. Her impressions seemed badly garbled, for she had so much to tell and could not keep the story straight. I could see that her mind was too full of all those terrible incidents to tell the story in chronological order. I had to piece it together from what she could tell me.

When the Russian Army invaded our hometown, the younger people fled out of town, but the older ones stayed there in the basements and air-raid shelter, where they were safer than being on the road. My mother, she told me, tried to walk out of town, after staying in the basement for some time. My mother was then almost seventy years of age and couldn't walk very fast; nevertheless, she walked about eight miles into a small village, where she was shot in the forehead by a Russian soldier. Nobody had the time or the courage to bury the dead, though some friends of ours brought back my mother's purse and kept it until my sister returned to town with her children, after fourteen days of wandering from farmer to farmer, begging for food and shelter. On her return to our town she found her house and our parents' house burned to the ground. Only a few survivors remained, and their ordeal was just beginning. My niece told me how my sister had to work for the Russian soldiers to get food for the children.

Hunger destroys human values. Some of the people in our town turned Communist as soon as the Russian Army entered the town, trying to be friendly with the soldiers. My family and the family of my sister were considered among the upper ten thousand, for we had four houses of our own, and my sister's husband was a jeweler and optician. My father's business was only a few blocks away, and our family was well known in the town. Those who sought to collaborate with the Communists told the Russian soldiers that my sister had diamonds and gold in her possession. The Russian state police took my sister and her children into custody, questioning her about the jewelry, finally beating her and confining her in prison. She and the children were displaced to Siberia, where my sister died of starvation after six months. My niece was kept in prison until 1949.

I promised my niece that I would take care of her, for I was the only male survivor of the family. Back on my job, my mind occupied with all these terrible experiences in our family, I found it difficult to work. Homeless, without friends, a stranger uprooted in West Germany—what future was there for me here? Perhaps I could start a new life in the United States; I determined to try. I went to the American Consulate and made my application to enter the United States as a refugee. I had to wait six years until my dream came true, six long years that seemed an eternity.

But now I am living in a free world, free of fear and anxiety, free of the past and looking forward toward a better and happy future. With all my heart and soul I can say, "God bless America."

CPSIA information can be obtained
at www.ICGtesting.com
Printed in the USA
BVOW06s1802180617

487206BV00008B/105/P

9 781258 141424